Essential Eight

LESSONS IN EXPERIENCING THE ABUNDANT LIFE

Pray 018
Salvation

Table of Contents

Essential Eight

How To Use This Study

Simple Steps to Getting Started

1. Find someone to do the study with you
2. Get a copy of this manual for each participant
3. Set up a time to meet weekly for eight weeks
4. Find the Essential Eight on KeryssoProject.com
5. Watch or listen to the lesson before you meet
6. Gather with your Faith Friend(s) and grow

Find Some Faith Friends

Jesus called us to be disciples who make disciples, and this study is designed to be a discipleship tool. Spiritual growth accelerates when you study with other believers. You spur each other to learn as you share the material and provide accountability to stay the course – as long as you both don't want to quit on the same day!

Look for one or two people who want to develop spiritually and increase in their knowledge of God's Word. Share this study with them and invite them to join with you for eight weekly meetings (either in person or online using a video conferencing app like Skype, Facetime, Zoom, etc.) Arrange a schedule, get this manual for everyone, and get going!

Lessons on Video and Audio

All eight of the lessons have been taught by various Kerysso Project teachers and are available as both audio and video recordings. These can be on our our website at KeryssoProject.com and are free of charge.

Before you meet to go over a lesson, each participant should listen to or watch the teaching for that week's lesson if possible. The recordings are no longer than 30 minutes, and they explain the lessons in detail by including illustrations and stories. If everyone listens to the lesson before you meet, you will all be prepared to have good discussion about the material.

Pointers for Your Meetings

Plan to meet for at least 40 minutes to give yourselves time to go through the study. Don't get distracted; stay with the material from the lesson. If there are other topics you want to discuss, set time aside for that, but dedicate at least 40 minutes to go over the material from the lesson.

Meet in a comfortable environment where you can freely share. Food always seems to enhance our fellowship, but don't let it get in the way of your purpose. If you meet in public, be sure to choose a place where you can hear each other and have personal conversation without worrying about who may be around you.

Go over the main points of the lesson. Someone may have a question or an insight to share. Then, go through the discussion questions, giving each person an opportunity to respond. When everyone has answered the questions, move on to the Big Daily Habit. Talk about how you can help each other develop the habit and make it part of your lives. Review the scripture from the Essential Words for the week. Recite last week's verse for each other. You may even come up with incentives for yourselves as you work to embrace these habits and memorize these scriptures. Make it fun!

Prayer should be part of each meeting. We haven't included specific prayer topics in each lesson, but Faith Friends pray for each other. It will be apparent as you meet what to pray for each other, but don't limit your prayers to requests and needs. Pray for growth. Pray that Christ will be fully formed within each of you and that He will manifest Himself through you to the people around you.

Questions to Discuss

At the end of each lesson, you'll find a list of questions to discuss. Determine to engage your heart as you talk through these subjects. When you have some Faith Friends who help you dig deeper into these questions, you'll find that your conversations will be richer and your faith will grow stronger. Don't skip or hurry through the questions. This is a vital part of going through this study!

Big Daily Habits

Each lesson in the Essential Eight is followed by a challenge for you to embrace a new daily habit. A Big Habit. Spiritual disciplines. These are practices that lead to growth and maturity in your life as a believer. People who lay down their lives and follow Jesus cultivate these habits and build their lives around them.

Don't think of these as laws to keep or rules to follow. Jesus won't love you any more if you do them – but you may love Him more as you develop your relationship with Him and come to know Him more. These habits serve as opportunities to yield yourself and focus on Him. Don't allow yourself to take on guilt or condemnation for what you don't do, but rejoice in what His grace empowers you to do.

If you miss a day (or a week), just start again the next day and keep going. Growing spiritually is a process we have to embrace. This is an investment. You are sowing seeds into your relationship with God. As you devote more time and attention to knowing Him, He will work in you and bring forth transformation from within you. Your thoughts and perspectives will change. You'll begin to look and sound more like Jesus. That's the goal of these habits - to be like Jesus.

Essential Words

We are challenging you to memorize a Bible verse from every lesson. The primary building material of a strong spiritual foundation is knowledge of God's Word.

As you hide these words in your heart and commit them to memory, they will become the base where your life in Christ stands and the grounding for what you produce.

God made promises to us concerning what His Word will produce in our lives. Here are some of those:

⊚ Psalm 119:11

Your word I have hidden in my heart, that I might not sin against You.

⊚ Proverbs 4:20-22

My son, give attention to my words; incline your ears to my sayings. Do not let them depart from your eyes; keep them in the midst of your heart; for they are life to those who find them, and health to all their flesh.

⊚ John 15:7

(Jesus said) "If you abide in Me, and My words abide in you, you will ask what you desire, and it shall be done for you."

Suggestions on how to memorize scripture:

⊚ Print the verse out on an index card that you carry with you and read several times a day or put it on your phone if you have it with you all day.

● Read the scripture aloud to yourself every morning and night. Keep this book by your bed so you can easily review the week's assignment.

● Hang all these verses on the mirror or near where you dress in the morning and read them over and over as you get ready for your day.

Knowing God

**The thief does not come except to
steal, and to kill, and to destroy. I have
come that they may have life, and that
they may have it more abundantly.**
John 10: 10

Jesus: The Express Image of God

Who is God? If we haven't seen Him, how can we
know Him? Religion offers many ideas of who God is, but
the Bible says He has chosen to reveal Himself through
His Son, Jesus.

In the past God spoke to our ancestors through
the prophets at many times and in various ways,
but in these last days he has spoken to us by his
Son, whom he appointed heir of all things, and
through whom also he made the universe. The

> Son is the radiance of God's glory and the exact representation of his being, sustaining all things by his powerful word...
> ● Hebrews 1:1-3a NIV

Jesus is the "exact representation" of God and His nature. He is the unseen God made visible to humanity.

> Christ is the visible image of the invisible God...
> ● Colossians 1:15a NLT

The Word was in the beginning, and the Word was God. The Word took on flesh as a man and lived here on Earth among people. Jesus is God incarnate (embodied in flesh, in human form), who came to us to show us the Father and declare Him to us.

> In the beginning was the Word, and the Word was with God, and the Word was God...And the Word became flesh and dwelt among us, and we beheld His glory, the glory as of the only begotten of the Father, full of grace and truth... No one has seen God at any time. The only begotten Son, who is in the bosom of the Father, He has declared Him.
> ● John 1:1, 14, 18

We can know the Father God through knowing Jesus because Jesus came to show us the Father. We know God's character from the character of Jesus. We know God's heart from the heart of Jesus.

"If you had known Me, you would have known My Father also; and from now on you know Him and have seen Him."
Philip said to Him, "Lord, show us the Father, and it is sufficient for us."
Jesus said to him, "Have I been with you so long, and yet you have not known Me, Philip? He who has seen Me has seen the Father; so how can you say, 'Show us the Father'?"
⊙ John 14:7-9

Our relationship with God is based fully on Jesus: who He was, what He did, what He reveals about God. We see Him, we see the Father.

Know God's Great Love For You

How you see God impacts everything in your life. Jesus showed us the Father as being good, benevolent, and loving. His nature is love. The greatest expression of His identity is that He is love.

He who does not love does not know God, for God is love.
⊙ 1 John 4:8

God's motivation in all He has done or will do is His love for you.

"For God so loved the world that He gave His only begotten Son, that whoever believes in Him should not perish, but have everlasting life."
◉ John 3:16

Jesus taught that the Father loves you as much as He loves Jesus.

"I am praying not only for these... but also for all who will ever believe in me because of their testimony...(that) the world will know that You sent Me and will understand that You love them as much as You love Me."
◉ John 17:20, 23b (NLT)

God demonstrated His love for us by sending Jesus to die on the cross as a sacrifice for our sins, to save us from sin and death.

But God demonstrates His own love toward us, in that while we were still sinners, Christ died for us.
◉ Romans 5:8

Through His love, we have become the children of God.

Behold what manner of love the Father has bestowed on us, that we should be called children of God!
◉ 1 John 3:1

Know the Life God Has For You

What we see Jesus doing for people in the Gospels is what He is still doing for people today: saving, healing, and delivering.

Jesus told us that He came (and that God sent Him) to give us life.

"The thief does not come except to steal, and to kill, and to destroy. I have come that they may have life, and that they may have it more abundantly."
◉ John 10:10

God is not a thief, a killer, or a destroyer. That's the enemy's work. God sent Jesus to make the way for you to live the abundant life.

◉ Abundant: excessive, overflowing, surplus, over and above, more than enough, profuse, extraordinary, above the ordinary, more than sufficient.

The abundant life in Christ is a life that supersedes the life you would normally live or the life you could make for yourself based on your own strength, ability, or means. It's an over-and-above life that overflows with God's goodness and is a higher, richer, better, fuller life than what you could ever have without Him.

There is a benefits package available for you as part of the abundant life in Christ.

> Bless the LORD, O my soul, And forget not all His benefits:
> Who forgives all your iniquities, Who heals all your diseases,
> Who redeems your life from destruction,
> Who crowns you with lovingkindness and tender mercies,
> Who satisfies your mouth with good things,
> So that your youth is renewed like the eagle's.
> ◉ Psalm 103:2-5

> Blessed be the God and Father of our Lord Jesus Christ, who has blessed us with every spiritual blessing in the heavenly places in Christ.
> ◉ Ephesians 1:3

> ... as His divine power has given to us all things that pertain to life and godliness...
> ◉ 2 Peter 1:3

Know Him For Yourself

Real life, eternal life, everlasting life – is knowing Him. This is our greatest privilege and best benefit in salvation. Jesus said so. The Apostle Paul agreed. Nothing else compares.

"And this is eternal life, that they may know You, the only true God, and Jesus Christ whom You have sent."
◉ John 17:3

...I also count all things loss for the excellence of the knowledge of Christ Jesus my Lord, for whom I have suffered the loss of all things, and count them as rubbish, that I may gain Christ... that I may know Him...
◉ Philippians 3:8, 10a

Our relationship with God starts with knowing Him through His Word. As we get to know His Word, we begin to see Him and believe that Jesus is the Christ. Through believing in Jesus and what He has done for us, we receive His life.

But these (the scriptures) are written that you may believe that Jesus is the Christ, the Son of God, and that believing you may have life in His name.
◉ John 20:31

Colossians 1:15 tells us that Christ is the visible image of the invisible God. What do we know about the nature and character of God based on what we see in Jesus?

Jesus declared in John 10:10 that He came to give us life while the enemy brings destruction. How does the truth that God is good and that He's offering you an abundant life challenge your perspective of God and what has happened in your life?

God loves us and wants us to know Him. How can you come to know Him in a greater way?

Read the Bible.

God chose to reveal Himself to us through His Word, and reading the scripture is the primary way we learn to know God. All that He is and all that He does aligns with His Word. We cannot really know Him without knowing the scripture.

You have many options for how you read the Bible, but choose a plan that you can actually do and incorporate into your daily life. You may want to read through the whole Bible in a year, but that requires reading 3-4 chapters every day and may not be something you can practically commit to do. If you aren't already reading daily, you probably shouldn't start with this.

Read for understanding and transformation. The goal is not to see how much you can accomplish but how much you can be impacted. Jesus said in John 8:32, "And you shall know the truth, and the truth shall make you free." You are reading to know the truth so that you can experience the freedom we have in Christ. Even if you only read a few verses each day, focus on what you read and ask the Holy Spirit to reveal the verses to you. Ask

Him how you can act on them and obey what He is saying to you.

Some options for Bible reading plans:

◉ Download the Bible app, and choose one of the many reading plans. The app does almost everything for you, except the reading – and it will even read the verses out loud to you!

◉ Commit to a timed period of reading, like 10 minutes first thing in the morning or before bed at night. This approach helps to take the emphasis off of how much you read and focuses you on understanding what you read.

◉ Pick a book of the Bible to read through. If you can read a study Bible or search on the internet, you will find background information on who wrote the book, to whom it was written, the circumstances under which it was written, etc. Many of the books of the New Testament were letters, and reading them through from end to end brings greater perspective to what the author has written.

◉ See the section at the end of this book called "How to Study the Bible" for more useful hints.

The thief does not come except to steal, and to kill, and to destroy. I have come that they may have life, and that they may have it more abundantly.

John 10:10

Essential Eight

The Good News of Jesus

For He made Him who knew no sin to be sin for us, that we might become the righteousness of God in Him.
2 Corinthians 5:21

First: The Bad News - Sin

According to the first chapters of Genesis, God's original plan for mankind was that we would live in fellowship with Him, free from sin and death, with no shame or guilt.

When man disobeyed God's command, he sinned. As a result, he lost his innocence, his acceptance, and his authority. Sin separated man from God, creating a gulf between man and God. Sin brought death upon man (which resulted in sickness, weakness, lack, poverty, strife, and eternal separation from God).

For the wages of sin is death...
◉ Romans 6:23

From that time forward, everyone who was born on earth was born into sin and was doomed to live under its curse. We had no escape.

Therefore, just as through one man (Adam) sin entered the world, and death through sin, and thus sin spread to all men, because all sinned...
◉ Romans 5:12

Because man was ashamed of his sinfulness and longed for what he lost through sin, he attempted to justify himself through good works and keeping the law. As he sought to regain what he had lost, man developed religion and other human philosophies to console himself and to, perhaps, earn his way back into all he had lost.

The sin problem remained, and the reign of sin left man condemned and spiritually dead (separated from the life of God and removed from fellowship with Him) with no hope of being restored.

Therefore, as through one man's offense judgment came to all men, resulting in condemnation...
◉ Romans 5:18a

Jesus Became Our Substitute at Calvary

Our sin demanded that we be punished by death. The only way out of sin and death was for someone else to take the punishment for our sins. Since every person was born stained with sin, there was no one to take our place. But God devised a plan to send His Son to be born of a virgin and fathered by God (and thereby untainted by sin). His Son, Jesus, lived a sinless life and qualified to be offered in our place as a sacrifice for us. JESUS BECAME OUR SUBSTITUTE.

> Surely He has borne our griefs and carried our sorrows; yet we esteemed His stricken, smitten by God, and afflicted. But He was wounded for our transgressions, He was bruised for our iniquities; the chastisement for our peace was upon Him, and by His stripes we are healed. All we like sheep have gone astray; we have turned, every one, to his own way; and the Lord has laid on Him the iniquity of us all.
> ◉ Isaiah 53:4-6

Jesus died our death on the cross, conquered death and hell, and rose from the dead. If we accept His sacrifice by faith, we have peace with God and are restored to fellowship with Him both now and for eternity.

Therefore, having been justified by faith, we have

peace with God through our Lord Jesus Christ.
 ◉ Romans 5:1

The Great Exchange

Jesus not only substituted Himself for us, but He also took on everything we had and everything we were. He then exchanged everything with us – He became what we were and made us into what He is.

> For you know the grace of our Lord Jesus Christ, that though He was rich, yet for your sakes, He became poor, that you through His poverty might become rich.
> ◉ 2 Corinthians 8:9

He took our sin and gave us His righteousness. Righteousness speaks of our good relationship and favored position with God. We are now righteous, which means we are right with God and in right-standing with Him. We can enjoy fellowship with Him.

> For He made Him who knew no sin to be sin for us that we might become the righteousness of God in Him.
> ◉ 2 Corinthians 5:21

Through becoming sin for us and making us righteous, Jesus has set us free from the dominion of sin and the death it brought. We no longer have to sin because we are no longer its slaves. And, because we are no longer counted guilty of sin, we aren't due any of the penalty of sin (spiritual death).

> Knowing this, that our old man was crucified with Him, that the body of sin might be done away with, that we should no longer be slaves of sin. For he who has died has been freed from sin. Now if we died with Christ, we believe that we shall also live with Him, knowing that Christ, having been raised from the dead, dies no more. Death no longer has dominion over Him.
> ◉ Romans 6:6-9

This is the good news for every believer: You now have the same position before God that Jesus has. Everything that Jesus did, you can do. All His rights and privileges are now your rights and privileges. For example, when you pray in His name, based on His Word, Heaven responds just as if Jesus Himself were making the request.

Your New Identity In Christ

Through accepting the sacrifice of Jesus, you entered into His death, burial, and resurrection. You died with Him and were resurrected with Him. The old you is dead, and a new you now lives in Christ.

> My old self has been crucified with Christ. It is no longer I who live, but Christ lives in me. So I

live in this earthly body by trusting in the Son of
God, who loved me and gave himself for me.
◉ Galatians 2:20 (NLT)

**In Christ you are a new person, a new creation. This
new you has a new identity, and the New Testament
(particularly the writings of Paul) gives you the
characteristics of your new identity. "In Christ", "in
Him," "in Whom," "by Him," "by Whom," "with Christ,"
and "with Him" are all phrases that speak of your new
identity in Christ.**

Therefore, if anyone is in Christ, he is a new
creation; old things have passed away; behold, all
things have become new.
◉ 2 Corinthians 5:17

**In Christ, you are privileged. You are seated with
Him in heavenly places (at the right hand of God in the
same position as Jesus) so that you can enjoy the
goodness of God firsthand and rule with Him.**

But God who is rich in mercy, because of His
great love with which He loved us, even when
we were dead in trespasses, made us alive
together with Christ [by grace you have been
saved], and raised us up together and made us sit
together in the heavenly places in Christ Jesus,
that in the ages to come He might show the
exceeding riches of His grace in His kindness

toward us in Christ Jesus.
  ◉ Ephesians 2:4-7

You are now a minister of reconciliation, an ambassador for Christ. You represent Him in this world. Your mission is to let Him use you to reach others with the Good News and reconcile them to God.

Now all things are of God, who has reconciled us to Himself through Jesus Christ, and has given us the ministry of reconciliation, that is, that God was in Christ reconciling the world to Himself, not imputing their trespasses to them, and has committed to us the word of reconciliation. Now then, we are ambassadors for Christ, as though God were pleading through us: we implore you on Christ's behalf, be reconciled to God.
  ◉ 2 Corinthians 5:18-20

The Good News is that God sent Jesus to pay the penalty for our sins and restore us to fellowship with Him. In what ways has sin affected life on Planet Earth and how has man responded to his sinfulness?

We see in 2 Corinthians 5:21 that Jesus took our place in sin and gave us His righteous position before the Father. How does having the same righteousness as Jesus benefit us?

Jesus made us new creations and gave us a new identity in Him. How will embracing your new identity in Christ change how you think about yourself and how you live?

Share Your Faith.

Jesus commissioned everyone who followed Him to go into their worlds and preach the Good News. This is not an option for believers; it is a mandate. It's part of your ministry as a believer to tell others about Jesus and what He has done.

What a privilege to work with God to reconcile and restore people to Him! He's chosen to work through ordinary people, empowering us to boldly share our faith and our story of His work in us. Obeying Him and reaching out to others will bring you great joy and your life will be richer in every way.

You were made to do this! Jesus said to those who followed Him, "I'll make you fishers of men." This is His work in you, but you choose whether you cooperate with Him. Do it! Let Him use you to reach your world.

⦿ Every morning, ask the Lord who He wants you to reach out to today. Consider the people who are already in your path: coworkers, fellow students, family members, friends, neighbors. Share the Good News of Jesus with the people you already know.

● Look for opportunities to have spiritual conversations. God is working with us, and He opens doors for us to share our faith. Be sensitive to people around you and recognize what He is doing and how He is drawing them.

● Use the script at the back of this book as a tool to reach others and preach the Gospel. If you aren't sure what to say or how to lead them to the Lord, the script will help. God wants to bring people into fellowship with Himself – and He wants to use you to do it!

For He made Him who knew no sin to be sin for us, that we might become the righteousness of God in Him.
● 2 Corinthians 5:21

A Life of Faith

For the just shall live by his faith in God...
Romans 1: 17

In God We Trust

Faith: TRUST, belief, confidence, conviction, reliance, persuasion.

As believers, we put our faith in God. To have faith in God is (1) to believe that God is who He says He is and (2) to trust Him to do what He has said He would do.

Faith in God is being convinced of His Word to the point that you are willing to act on it or depend on it as truth.

⊚ "Faith isn't faith until it acts on what it believes."

- Smith Wigglesworth

To have faith in the Bible (God's Word) is to read it as if its promises were written to you by the most trustworthy person you know.

If you can trust people, then you are capable of having faith in God. How much more does He deserve our trust?

Saved By Grace Through Faith

To receive salvation, the only thing required of us was faith. God did all the work for us, and we get all of the benefits. Our part is having faith (believing and acting on what He has said).

For by grace you have been saved through faith, and that not of yourselves, it is the gift of God, not of works, lest anyone should boast.
⊚ Ephesians 2:8-9

We were saved by grace. Grace is unmerited favor. We didn't do anything to deserve salvation, nor have we earned it in any way, but He gave us salvation as a free gift because He loved us.

Even the faith which we use to connect to Him is a gift from Him. Faith rises in our hearts as we hear His Word.

> So then faith comes by hearing and hearing by
> the Word of God.
> ◉ Romans 10:17

Faith is actually encapsulated in God's Word. When you hear His Word (or read it because then you "hear" it in your mind) and receive it, faith is deposited in your heart.

When you heard and received the Gospel, those words went into you and began to persuade your heart to believe. Faith arose from within you.

Because faith comes by hearing God's Word, to have faith in God for something, you have to have His Word on it. You have to know His will on the subject. Your faith can only begin when His will is known.

Continually Receive From God Through Faith

Salvation is the benefit package that contains everything that Jesus has so generously provided for us. He anticipated all we would need and has already granted to us all that is necessary to live for Him.

> By his divine power, God has given us everything we need for living a godly life. We have received all of this by coming to know him, the one who called us to himself by means of his marvelous glory and excellence.
> ◉ 2 Peter 1:3 (NLT)

The way we initially received salvation is the same way receive everything that has been provided for us in salvation. We receive from Him by grace, through faith.

How exactly are we saved?

> ...the word is near you, in your mouth and in your heart (that is, the word of faith which we preach): that if you confess with your mouth the Lord Jesus and believe in your heart that God has raised Him from the dead, you will be saved. For with the heart one believes unto righteousness, and with the mouth confession is made unto salvation.
> ◉ Romans 10:8-10

Heart: Believe the Gospel (the death, burial, and resurrection of Jesus)
Mouth: Confess (declare that you agree with) the Lord Jesus

To receive what God has promised us, we believe what His Word says, and we declare that we agree with it.

For example, to receive the peace that Jesus gave us:

First, believe what Jesus said in John 14:27:
"Peace I leave with you, My peace I give to you; not as the world gives do I give to you. Let not your heart be troubled, neither let it be afraid."
Second, declare that you agree with it:
"I believe that Jesus has given me His peace. I have His peace. I won't let my heart be troubled, nor will I be afraid."

The Exercise of Faith

Faith is our response to what God has already done-- believing in the accomplished, finished, complete work of Christ on the cross. Through that work, He purchased our redemption, paid for our freedom, and provided for our victory in every situation.

Agree with God's Word.

The word that saves is right here, as near as the tongue in your mouth, as close as the heart in your chest. It's the word of faith that welcomes God to go to work and set things right for us. This is the core of our preaching. Say the welcoming word to God—"Jesus is my Master"— embracing, body and soul, God's work of doing in us what he did in raising Jesus from the dead.

That's it. You're not "doing" anything; you're simply calling out to God, trusting him to do it for you. That's salvation. With your whole being you embrace God setting things right, and then you say it, right out loud: "God has set everything right between him and me!"
◉ Romans 10:8-10 (MSG)

The same way you are saved is the same way you appropriate God's saving work in every area of your life.

You don't have to talk God into anything. You just have to agree with what He's already said.

Remember, your life reveals what is in your heart. What you say and what you do reflects what you believe.

The Challenge to Faith

Our faith in God is not based on what our physical senses perceive but on what He says to us in His Word. The biggest challenge of faith is getting past your dependence on your senses and learning to trust in someone you cannot see with your natural eyes

For we walk by faith, not by sight.
◉ 2 Corinthians 5:7

Just because you can't see something doesn't mean it doesn't exist.

By faith we understand that the world was created by the word of God, so that what is seen was made out of things which do not appear.
● Hebrews 11:3 (RSV)

To live by faith, you have to trust in a God whom you don't see but who is definitely real.

Now faith is the turning of dreams into deeds; it is betting your life on the unseen realities.
● Hebrews 11:1 (Cotton Patch Translation)

If you are struggling to trust God in some area, you need to let God's Word persuade your heart. If you will continue to hear His Word about a subject, faith will come and be deposited in your heart. As you hear and hear, faith will begin to rise from within you. You will begin to "see the unseen" and the words that flow from your heart will soon agree with that unseen reality. Your actions will then follow, and you will start to actually rely on God's Word as the truth. Then, you will be living by faith!

Questions to Discuss

Faith is a word many use to describe a belief system, but we have faith in God and what He has done for us in Christ. How do we put our faith in God and enter into a relationship with Him?

Ephesians 2 says that we are saved by grace, through faith. How does this differ from earning God's approval through our own good works?

In Romans 1:17, we see that we are called to live by faith in God. How can you grow in your reliance on God and live your life by faith in a greater way?

Declare God's Word.

Romans 10:17 tells us that faith comes from hearing God's Word. As we speak His Word, our ears hear what we are saying and it goes down into our hearts. When we accept it and let it take root in us, His Word begins to produce faith in us, enabling us to receive from God.

When we agree with what the scriptures say, we are giving God the authority to bring those words to pass in our lives. We are yielding to Him and allowing Him to have free reign within us. As we give our consent, the power in His Words is released, transforming us and our worlds.

Declaring God's Word in the name of Jesus is like Jesus Himself speaking. All of heaven is backing you up, ready to move on your behalf. Fill your mouth with His Word, and you will get the same results He did.

○ Find scriptures that address who you are and what you've been given in Christ, and print them out. Hang these on your mirror so that you can speak them over yourself as you dress for your day or put them over your desk where you work.

● Take the promises God made or the commands He gave us and carry them with you during the day on cards or in your phone. When you have a free moment, pull these out and read them aloud quietly to yourself (if you are around people). Aim to do this twice a day.

● Prepare a list of scriptures (or find one online) to declare over your life and household daily during your devotional time. Gather your children and lead them in these declarations. Take turns leading each other in these as you drive or before dinner or bedtime.

That if you confess with your mouth the Lord Jesus and believe in your heart that God has raised Him from the dead, you will be saved. For with the heart one believes unto righteousness, and with the mouth confession is made unto salvation.

● Romans 10:9-10

Fellowship with the Father

Now this is the confidence that we have in Him, that if we ask anything according to His will, He hears us. And if we know that He hears us, whatever we ask, we know that we have the petitions that we have asked of Him.
1 John 5:14-15

We Have the Privilege of Prayer

The purpose of Jesus restoring us to God, making us right with Him and giving us His position before the Father is so that we can fellowship with Our Heavenly Father. This was what He originally intended for us, and

He longs to have a close, intimate relationship with each of us.

Prayer is communing with God, inquiring of Him, making requests of Him, sharing with Him, partnering with Him, listening to Him, worshipping Him, receiving from Him, and drawing close to Him.

We have nothing to fear as we approach God. Through Christ, we have free access to His throne, where we can receive whatever we may need from God. Because of His grace, we can come to Him without reservation and be accepted like Jesus Himself.

> Let us therefore come boldly to the throne of grace, that we may obtain mercy and find grace to help in time of need.
> ◉ Hebrews 4:16

> ◉ "Prayer is no dreary performance, dead and death-dealing, but it is God's enabling act for man, living and life-giving, joy and joy-giving. Prayer is the contact of a living soul with God. In prayer, God stoops to kiss man, to bless man, and to aid man in everything that God can devise or man can need."
> - E. M. Bounds

The Basics of Prayer

Most people pray based on what they have heard others pray. Much of what we practice as prayer is based on religious traditions.

God gave us the Bible as His instructions to us, a manual for living. The scripture serves as a guidebook on prayer.

Always launch your prayers from the platform of God's Word. This is the key to having your prayers answered. If what we ask is based on His Word, He hears us, and then we know that we have it.

> Now this is the confidence that we have in Him, that if we ask anything according to His will, He hears us. And if we know that He hears us, whatever we ask, we know that we have the petitions that we have asked of Him.
> ◉ 1 John 5:14-15

Find scriptures that address your particular need or circumstance, and then pray based on those scriptures. For example: When you don't know what to do, remind yourself (and God) of James 1:5, where He promised to give you wisdom. Then ask Him for it, and thank Him for giving it to you.

> If any of you lacks wisdom, let him ask of God, who gives to all liberally and without reproach, and it will be given to him.
> ◎ James 1:5

Our authority in prayer is based on what Jesus did for us and whom He made us to be. We pray in the name of Jesus, and it is as if Jesus Himself is making the request. He gave us His power of attorney.

> "And whatever you ask in My name, that I will do, that the Father may be glorified in the Son. If you ask anything in My name, I will do it."
> ◎ John 14:13-14

When you spend time with God and take advantage of the privilege of prayer, anxiety and worry will depart from you, and God's peace will stand guard over your heart and mind.

> Be anxious for nothing, but in everything by prayer and supplication, with thanksgiving, let your requests be made known to God, and the peace of God, which surpasses all understanding, will guard your hearts and minds through Christ Jesus.
> ◎ Philippians 4:6

Various Types of Prayers

Prayer of Consecration: a prayer to dedicate your life to God's use. This should be the constant prayer of every follower of Christ. Note that when Jesus consecrated Himself in the Garden of Gethsemane, He prayed, "if it is Your will." This is the only time we see this phrase used in prayer because as we give ourselves to God, we don't always fully know all the facets of God's specific plans for us.

> "Father, if it is Your will, take this cup away from Me; nevertheless, not My will, but Yours be done."
> ◎ Luke 22:42

Prayer of Faith: a prayer of petition to receive what God has already promised and provided for us in His Word. When you see something God has promised us in the scripture, ask Him for that to be done in your life, believe He grants your request when you pray, and then thank Him for honoring His promise to you.

> "Therefore I say to you, whatever things you ask when you pray, believe that you receive them, and you will have them."
> ◎ Mark 11:24

Prayer of Agreement: to join with another believer of like faith in prayer and agree (say the same thing) together on what God's Word promises you. When you are overwhelmed by life and struggling, find someone strong in faith to join together with you in prayer. This strengthens you and enables you to stand steadfast.

> "Again, I say to you that if two of you agree on earth concerning anything that they ask, it will be done for them by my Father in Heaven."
> ◉ Matthew 18:19

Prayer of Supplication: a prayer for fellow believers, praying that their needs will be met or that they will fulfill God's plans and purposes for them. We are admonished to pray for one another, and the New Testament (particularly in Paul's epistles) offers many examples of these prayers.

> Therefore I also, after I heard of your faith in the Lord Jesus and your love for all the saints, do not cease to give thanks for you, making mention of you in my prayers: that the God of our Lord Jesus Christ, the Father of glory, may give to you the spirit of wisdom and revelation in the knowledge of Him, the eyes of your understanding being enlightened; that you may know what is the hope of His calling, what are the riches of the glory of His inheritance in the saints, and what is the exceeding greatness of His power toward us who believe, according to the working of His mighty power...
> ◉ Ephesians 1:15-19

For this reason we also, since the day we heard it, do not cease to pray for you, and to ask that you may be filled with the knowledge of His will in all wisdom and spiritual understanding; that you may walk worthy of the Lord, fully pleasing Him, being fruitful in every good work and increasing in the knowledge of God; strengthened with all might, according to His glorious power, for all patience and longsuffering with joy; giving thanks to the Father who has qualified us to be partakers of the inheritance of the saints in the light.
● Colossians 1:9-12

Also read Philippians 1:9-11 and Ephesians 3:14-21.

Prayer of Intercession: a prayer for the lost that stands in the gap between them and God, praying what they cannot pray for themselves. The prayer for the Lord of the Harvest to send laborers into His harvest from Matthew 9:36-38 is an example of this.

Praise and Worship: these are prayers that magnify God, boast of Him, celebrate and exalt Him, reverence and adore Him. These may be prayed or set to music and sung. See Hebrews 13:15.

Prayer in the Spirit: praying in tongues, inspired by the Holy Spirit. This kind of prayer enables us to pray

God's perfect will when we aren't sure how to pray according to Romans 8:26.

Jesus made the way for us to fellowship with Our Heavenly Father. What privileges do we have in prayer because of what Jesus did for us?

The Bible is our prayer manual. What does it tell us about how to be effective when we pray and how to receive answers to our prayers?

The scriptures shows us different kinds of prayer that we should pray. How can you embrace these to expand your prayer life and grow in your fellowship with the Father?

Fellowship with the Father.

The Father's heart is towards His children, and He longs to fellowship with us. Jesus made this possible by cleansing us from our sins and raising us to the same position with God that He enjoys. We now have the privilege of drawing near to God, talking to Him, sharing His heart, and making requests of Him.

Start your day by spending time with God--not because you *should,* but because you *can.* Close fellowship in a relationship is dependent upon maintaining intimacy. Just as you would check in with your spouse in the morning, talking to your Heavenly Father is key to your relationship with Him.

Knowing that the God of the universe is just a whisper away gives you great peace and confidence. He's on your side, and you have the authority to bring His power on the scene. Prayer is your connection to Him, and constant communion keeps you in step with Him.

◉ First thing in the morning, pray. Talk to God. Thank Him for who He is and who He's made you to be. Thank Him for taking care of you.

Remind Him and yourself what His Word says about anything that's concerning you. End your day the same way.

◉ Take advantage of times in your day when you are alone (when you're driving or in the shower, for example). Pray and worship the Lord. Open your heart and talk to Him.

◉ Paul said to pray without ceasing – so do that. Check in with Him throughout your day.

Now this is the confidence that we have in Him, that if we ask anything according to His will, He hears us. And if we know that He hears us, whatever we ask, we know that we have the petitions that we have asked of Him.

◉ 1 John 5:14-15

The Baptism of the Holy Spirit

"But you shall receive power when the Holy Spirit has come upon you; and you shall be witnesses to Me in Jerusalem, and in all Judea and Samaria, and to the end of the earth."
Acts 1: 8

The Promise of the Holy Spirit

The plan of God was to bring Jesus to heaven after His Resurrection. Before He ascended, Jesus told His disciples that the Father was going to send the Holy Spirit to help them and live with them forever.

"And I will pray the Father, and He will give you another Helper (Comforter, one called to Help) that He may abide with you forever."
⊚ John 14:16

Jesus was saying here that the Father will send "one besides Me and in addition to Me but one just like Me. He will do in My absence what I would do if I were physically present with you."
⊚ Word Wealth, Spirit Filled Life Bible

Though difficult to believe, Jesus said it is actually better for us to have the Holy Spirit than to have Jesus here with us personally in the flesh.

"Nevertheless, I tell you the truth. It is to your advantage that I go away; for if I do not go away, the Helper will not come to you; but if I depart, I will send Him to you."
⊚ John 16:7

Until this point, Jesus' followers had looked to Him to meet their needs, to dispense God's power, and to speak for God. Jesus was introducing a new way God wanted to work: not just through one person (as He did in Jesus), but through many persons (as He could if He empowered others in the same way that He had Jesus).

And being assembled together with them, He commanded them not to depart from Jerusalem, but to wait for the Promise of the Father, "which," He said, "you have heard from Me; for John truly baptized with water, but you shall be baptized with the Holy Spirit not many days from now." "But YOU shall receive power when the Holy Spirit has come upon you; and you shall be witnesses to Me in Jerusalem, and in all Judea and Samaria, and to the end of the earth."

◎ Acts 1:4-5, 8

The reason for the Holy Spirit coming upon us is so that we can receive power - the same power His followers had seen on Him. The foremost reason for the power of God coming upon you is so that you can be a witness (someone who can produce evidence.) God never intended that we reach people only through persuasive words, but He sent us His Spirit so we would have power in our lives to bear witness of Him.

What is the Baptism of the Holy Spirit??

Baptize: to immerse. When you are baptized in water, you are immersed in water. When you are baptized in the Holy Spirit, you are immersed in Him.

When you are born again, the Holy Spirit comes to live inside you. When you are baptized in the Holy Spirit, He fills you completely with Himself and comes up from within you, out up-on you.

The Baptism in the Holy Spirit is the experience of having the Spirit of God immerse you and fill you to overflowing until He affects your flesh. Salvation produces a fountain of water springing up within you, but the baptism of the Holy Spirit brings forth rivers of living water flowing out of your innermost being.

> "But the water that I give him will become in him a fountain of water springing up into everlasting life."
> ◉ John 4:14b

> "...out of His heart will flow rivers of living water."
> ◉ John 7:38b

The Baptism of the Holy Spirit is a manifestation of God's Spirit that produces supernatural (beyond the natural) experiences in people. In the Bible, when believers were baptized in the Holy Spirit, they spoke in other tongues as the Holy Spirit enabled them.

> When the Day of Pentecost had fully come, they were all with one accord in one place. And suddenly there came a sound from heaven, as of a rushing mighty wind, and it filled the whole house where they were sitting. Then there appeared to them divided tongues, as of fire, and one sat upon each of them. And they were all filled with the Holy Spirit and began to speak with other tongues, as the Spirit gave them utterance.
> ◉ Acts 2:1-4

We see in Acts that this baptism is an experience that comes after salvation. When Peter and John went to Samaria, they found people who had already received the word of God and been baptized in the name of Jesus (referring to water baptism), but when the apostles laid hands on them, they received the Baptism of the Holy Spirit.

> Now when the apostles who were at Jerusalem heard that Samaria had received the word of God, they sent Peter and John to them, who, when they had come down, prayed for them that they might receive the Holy Spirit. For as yet He had fallen upon none of them. They had only been baptized in the name of the Lord Jesus. Then they laid hands on them, and they received the Holy Spirit.
> ◉ Acts 8:14-17

Why Speak in Other Tongues?

Tongues are the initial sign of the baptism of the Holy Spirit. In Acts 2, when the Holy Spirit was first poured out, the first indication that something had happened in them was that people heard them speaking in tongues which are languages they don't know or understand.

> While Peter was still speaking these words, the Holy Spirit fell upon all those who heard the

word. And those of the circumcision who believed were astonished, as many as came with Peter, because the gift of the Holy Spirit had been poured out on the Gentiles also. For they heard them speak with tongues and magnify God.
⊜ Acts 10:44-46

Praying in the Spirit, or speaking in tongues, is a supernatural experience. When you do this, you are praying in languages unknown to you. You are in direct contact with God, talking about things that no one understands, not even you. The scripture says that the things you are praying are considered to be mysteries and divine secrets.

For he who speaks in a tongue does not speak to men but to God, for no one understands him; however, in the spirit he speaks mysteries.
⊜ 1 Corinthians 14:2

Speaking in tongues edifies and energizes the believer. It's a way we can be refreshed and recharged and be strengthened in our faith.

He who speaks in a tongue edifies [to charge like a battery] himself.
⊜ 1 Corinthians 14:4

Praying in tongues allows us to pray in alignment with God's will. When we don't know God's will in a situation because it's not specifically revealed in His

Word or when we don't know the particular details of a situation, we can pray in the Holy Spirit and be sure we are praying what God would have us pray.

> Likewise the Spirit also helps in our weaknesses. For we do not know what we should pray for as we ought, but the Spirit Himself makes intercession for us with groanings which cannot be uttered (referring to tongues). Now He who searches the hearts knows what the mind of the Spirit is, because He makes intercession for the saints according to the will of God.
> ◉ Romans 8:26-27

You Can Receive the Baptism of the Holy Spirit

The Holy Spirit is a gift from the Father. To receive, you simply ask Him to baptize you in the Holy Spirit and receive by faith. Then, yield yourself to Him, allowing Him to fill you, and speak out by faith.

> "If you then, being evil, know how to give good gifts to your children, how much more will your heavenly Father give the Holy Spirit to those who ask Him!"
> ◉ Luke 11:13

Jesus told His followers in Acts 1:8 that they would receive power from the Holy Spirit. What does the empowerment of the Holy Spirit do in our lives and what is its purpose?

In Acts 8, Peter and John introduced the baptism of the Holy Spirit to people who had already received Jesus. How does the baptism in the Holy Spirit differ from receiving Jesus (being born again)?

The baptism of the Holy Spirit is the Father's gift to us. How can you receive more benefit from this precious gift in your life?

Pray in Tongues.

One great privilege of being baptized in the Holy Spirit is being enabled to speak in other tongues (also called praying in the Spirit.) As the Holy Spirit allows us to utter words that we don't understand, we are praying in perfect agreement with God's will without tainting it by our own thoughts and desires. We are also declaring divine secrets as we pray in ways we would never be able to from our own minds.

Developing the habit of praying in tongues everyday helps you grow spiritually. For those moments you are speaking in tongues, you are yielding your mouth to God and allowing Him to speak through you. Yielding your voice to Him opens the door for you to allow Him to have His way in others areas of your life.

Praying in the Spirit is supernatural. You can't make up enough syllables or sustain these languages for a significant period of time in your own human ability. The time you devote to this brings forth the rivers of living water from within you, and they will continue to flow throughout your day. Do this every day, and you will experience God's power in greater ways all through your life.

● Start your day by praying in the Spirit. Make it part of your devotional time if you have one. If not, pray as you shower, dress, drive, and get going on your day.

● Pray in tongues quietly to yourself as you go through your day. Because your mind isn't engaged in this, you can do it while you work or complete other tasks.

● Any time you feel anxious, overwhelmed, or tired, pray in the Spirit. This practice will charge you up and bring you into God's peace.

But you shall receive power when the Holy Spirit has come upon you; and you shall be witnesses to Me in Jerusalem, and in all Judea and Samaria, and to the end of the earth.
● Acts 1:8

The Leading of the Holy Spirit

However, when He, the Spirit of truth, has come, He will guide you into all truth; for He will not speak on His own authority, but whatever He hears He will speak; and He will tell you things to come.
John 16: 13

The Holy Spirit: God's Guide In Us

A marvelous result of the New Birth is that God came to live in man. Under the Old Covenant (in the Old Testament), God only worked through the priest, prophet, or king. And, He came upon them only for a moment. The common man had no hope of contact with God.

Jesus made it possible for the Holy Spirit to come live within us. He now serves as our inner guide. Jesus said:

> "However, when He, the Spirit of Truth, has come, He will guide you into all truth...and He will tell you things to come."
> ◉ John 16:13

Learn to Follow His Leading

Learning to follow the leading of the Holy Spirit is a process. You can come to His voice for yourself and grow in your ability to discern what He is saying and where He is guiding.

The first step in learning His leading is to follow the written Word. The Holy Spirit always leads us in ways that agree with the Scriptures. He never tells us to do anything contrary to His Word.

> Your Word is a lamp unto my feet and a light unto my path.
> ◉ Psalm 119:105

As you endeavor to obey His general direction in the written Word, the Holy Spirit will begin to reveal the

Scriptures to you and give you more specific direction for your life.

Know that God communicates with us spirit to spirit, not through our minds or bodies. His Spirit lives in our spirits, and that is where He speaks to us. Don't look for Him to speak to your physical senses (like in an audible voice). Listen for Him on the inside, in your spirit.

> The spirit of man is the lamp of the Lord...
> ◉ Proverbs 20:27

The Holy Spirit is ever leading us into all the benefits that God provided for us in salvation, the benefits we can enjoy as children of God. He leads us into the fullness of His good plan for us. If we fail to follow Him, we'll miss out on what God has for us.

> For as many as are led by the Spirit of God, these
> are the sons [and daughters] of God.
> ◉ Romans 8:14

Hearing God is much simpler than you may imagine it to be. If you have an assurance of salvation (a knowing that you belong to Him), then you are hearing from God. As He leads us in our daily lives, His Spirit bears witness with our spirit and verifies on the inside that we are doing the right thing or going the right way.

> The Spirit Himself bears witness with our spirit

that we are children of God.
● Romans 8:16

He Leads Us by Peace

The best way to make sure you are following the leading of the Holy Spirit is to follow peace. Establish peace in your life, and when you make decisions, look for it. Let peace rule on your choices.

And let the peace... from Christ rule (act as umpire continually) in your hearts (deciding and settling with finality all questions that arise in your minds...)
● Colossians 3:15 (AMPC)

To make sure you are following peace, start out by taking non-committal baby steps. If you have peace there, take another step. At each move, check your peace level. Don't override your peace or let people or time bully you into decisions. Follow peace!

When the Holy Spirit is leading you, it just seems right down on the inside. Your peace isn't based on reason or logic. Luke, the writer of Acts, expressed the leading of the Holy Spirit in these words:

...it seemed good...
● Acts 15:34

Any leading you have from the Holy Spirit – even if you have peace - should be judged in light of the written Word. The Bible is the final authority. The Holy Spirit will always agree with (say the same thing as) the Word.

> Test all things. Hold fast what is good.
> ◉ 1 Thessalonians 5:21

Ways the Holy Spirit Does NOT Lead Us

God does not lead His people by circumstances (like open doors/closed doors). In the Old Testament, since God had no way to communicate spirit-to-spirit with people, the only way He could speak to them was through natural circumstances. However, Jesus made it possible for His Spirit to live within us.

Never in the New Testament are we taught to ask for a natural sign to indicate God's will for us. Instead, we are taught to live by the inward witness. In Acts 1, the eleven remaining disciples cast lots to decide who would replace Judas. Once the Holy Spirit came upon them in Acts 2, never again was this practice mentioned. They no longer needed to cast lots because they had the Holy Spirit on the inside to guide them.

> And they cast their lots, and the lot fell on Matthias. And he was numbered with the eleven apostles.
> ◉ Acts 1:26

The Holy Spirit does not lead through prophecy [a God-inspired utterance] given by another person or even a minister. That is not the New Testament purpose for prophecy; prophecy is for edification [charging up like a battery] and exhortation and comfort.

> ...he who prophesies speaks edification and exhortation and comfort to men.
> ◉ 1 Corinthians 14:3

The Holy Spirit Leads Us to Be His Witnesses

The goal of all His guidance in our lives is for us to work with Him to accomplish His plans in the Earth. His assignment for all of us is to preach the Gospel and be His witnesses wherever we go.

> "But you shall receive power when the Holy Spirit has come upon you; and you shall be witnesses to Me in Jerusalem, and in all Judea and Samaria, and to the end of the earth."
> ◉ Acts 1:8

As we learn to listen to Him, the Holy Spirit will give us the words we need to speak for Him as His representatives.

> "Now when they bring you to the synagogues and magistrates and authorities, do not worry about how or what you should answer, or what

you should say. For the Holy Spirit will teach you
in
that very hour what you ought to say."
⊙ Luke 12:11-12

Throughout the New Testament, we see the Holy Spirit leading believers into ministry opportunities and opening doors for them to reach people with the Good News. He is still leading His people today for the same purpose. He is leading you, if you will hear Him and follow!

Some don't think God speaks today, but the scripture teaches otherwise. How does God communicate with people, and how do we know He is leading us?

Colossians 3:15 tells us to let the peace of God rule and settle all questions that arise in our lives. How do we allow His peace to determine the steps we take in life?

Learning to follow the leading of the Holy Spirit is a process. It is a lifelong pursuit. What are steps you can take towards following His leading in a greater way?

Listen for His Leading.

The Holy Spirit is always doing His job, leading us into what God has for us, but we aren't always in tune with Him. The cares of life often distract us and draw our attention to this natural realm. If we are going to hear from Heaven, we have to be intentional about listening for His voice.

Hearing from God is not natural for humans, but it should become normal for us as believers. If you purposely look inside as you go about your day, you will begin to pick up on His leading. You will start to sense Him guiding you and showing you what to do.

The more you endeavor to follow Him, the stronger His gentle nudges will become. You'll sense when your peace is disturbed or feel Him urging you to do something. It takes practice, but if you check with Him throughout your day, you will get to know His voice and be sure He is speaking to you.

● When you pray, take a few moments to quiet yourself and listen on the inside. Prayer isn't one-sided with you doing all the talking. See if He has a response to you.

● Praying in the Spirit helps you be more spiritually sensitive. His leading comes from the same place that your prayer language does. Tune in there to hear from Him.

● Check-in with Him throughout your day. How is your peace level? If you find your peace is disturbed in some way, take a moment to pray and discern how He is leading.

However, when He, the Spirit of truth, has come, He will guide you into all truth; for He will not speak on His own authority, but whatever He hears He will speak; and He will tell you things to come.
● John 16:13

Healing Belongs To You

How God anointed Jesus of Nazareth with the Holy Spirit and with power, who went about doing good and healing all who were oppressed by the devil, for God was with Him.
Acts 10:38

Healing Is God's Will For You

Many people are unsure of God's will to heal. They seek to determine God's will based on experience or tradition, but we can't look to these to see God's plans. How can we be sure of God's will? God gave us His Word to reveal His will to us.

As we study the scripture, there are three places we can look to see God's perfect will for man: the Garden of Eden (before the fall), Heaven, and the ministry of Jesus.

In the first chapters of Genesis, when the Garden is described, there is no mention of any sickness or disease. God created man according to His own will and purpose. If He had wanted man sick, He would have made Him sick from the beginning. It was Adam's sin that opened him (and thus all humanity) to the curse of sickness.

> For the wages of sin is death.
> ◎ Romans 6:23

In the scriptures that refer to Heaven, no one there is depicted as sick or infirm. In what we call The Lords' Prayer, we see two truths concerning the will of God. 1) The will of God is done in Heaven. 2) The will of God is not necessarily being done on earth. If God's will was automatically being done, there would have been no need for Jesus to pray this.

> (Jesus prayed) "Your will be done on earth as it is in Heaven."
> ◎ Matthew 6:10

There is no record in the Gospels that Jesus ever told anyone who came to Him to be healed, "No, you can't be healed because it's not God's will for you to be healed." Jesus came to show us the Father. His ministry is proof of God's will to heal.

> "For I have come down from Heaven, not to do My own will, but the will of Him who sent Me."
> ◎ John 6:38

Jesus came to do the will of the Father. He freely dispensed the healing power of God, healing every sickness and every disease.

> Then Jesus went about all the cities and villages, teaching in their synagogues, preaching the gospel of the kingdom, and healing every sickness and every disease among the people.
> ◎ Matthew 9:35

Jesus forever settled the question of whether it is God's will to heal. A leper came to Him and questioned His willingness to heal. Jesus responded firmly and answered, "I will," and then healed him.

> When He had come down from the mountain, great multitudes followed Him. And behold, a leper came and worshiped Him, saying, "Lord, if you are willing, You can make me clean." Then Jesus put out His hand and touched him, saying, "I am willing; be cleansed." Immediately his leprosy was cleansed.
> ◎ Matthew 8:1-3

Sickness Comes From satan

Sickness came as a part of the death that sin brought. It's from the devil. In fact, the Bible calls sickness an oppression of the devil.

How God anointed Jesus of Nazareth with the
Holy Spirit and with power, who went about
doing good and healing all who were oppressed
of the devil, for God was with Him.
  ◉ Acts 10:38

**When Jesus saw a woman bent over who couldn't
raise herself up, it made Him angry. He immediately
assigned blame for her bondage to satan and declared
that she should be set free.**

"So ought not this woman, being a daughter of
Abraham, whom Satan has bound – think of it –
for eighteen years, be loosed from this bond on
the Sabbath?"
  ◉ Luke 13:16

**Jesus alerted us to the intentions of the enemy.
Sickness is one tool that the devil uses to steal, kill and
destroy. It's definitely a contradiction to the abundant
life that Jesus came to give us.**

"The thief does not come except to steal, and to
kill, and to destroy. I have come that they may
have life and that they may have it more
abundantly."
  ◉ John 10:10

Jesus Paid For Our Healing and Gave It To Us

Because sickness came on mankind as a result of Adam's sin, someone had to pay the penalty and bear the punishment to redeem us out from under sin and all that came on us as a result of sin, including sickness. That's what Jesus did when He suffered, bled, and died at Calvary. The stripes on His back paid for our healing.

> Surely He has borne our griefs (sicknesses, weaknesses, and distresses) and carried our sorrows and pains [of punishment], yet we [ignorantly] considered Him stricken, smitten, and afflicted by God [as if with leprosy]. But He was wounded for our transgressions, He was bruised for our guilt and iniquities; the chastisement [needful to obtain] peace and well-being for us was upon Him, and with the stripes [that wounded] Him we are healed and made whole.
> ◉ Isaiah 53:4-5 (AMPC)

> He Himself took our infirmities and bore our sicknesses.
> ◉ Matthew 8:17b

> By His stripes, you were healed [Greek: physically healed].
> ◉ 1 Peter 2:24

69

You are not a sick person trying to get your healing. Your healing is an accomplished fact; it was settled at the cross. When you were born again, you received in your salvation package a benefit called healing, and now it belongs to you. You are entitled to it.

Healing cannot be earned any more than any other part of salvation can. Healing comes by grace, through faith, just as every benefit of your salvation. It is God's gift to you, given because He loves you.

Receive healing in your body by going to the scriptures that promise you healing, laying hold of your healing by faith, and thanking God for it. If you are struggling to receive, you can call on the spiritual leaders of the church to minister healing to you, and you'll be made well.

> Is anyone among you sick? Let him call for the elders of the church, and let them pray over him, anointing him with oil in the name of the Lord. 15 And the prayer of faith will save the sick, and the Lord will raise him up...
> ◉ James 5:14-15a

Jesus Commissioned Us to Heal the Sick

Healing the sick is part of our ministry as believers. He gave The Great Commission to those who followed Him (we're included as part of this commission.) He told us to go and preach the Gospel. He also said to lay hands on the sick, they would recover, and these healings would confirm the Gospel we preach. As the believers obeyed His command, the Lord honored His Word, working with them and bringing forth healings and miracles.

"Go into all the world and preach the gospel... lay hands on the sick and they will recover... And they went out and preached everywhere, the Lord working with them and confirming the word through the accompanying signs."
☉ Mark 16:15, 18b, 20

When Jesus sent out the twelve disciples, He gave them the equipment they would need to minister effectively. He empowered them to cast out the devil and to heal any sickness and diseases they encountered. He did the same when He sent out the seventy.

And when He had called His twelve disciples to Him, He gave them power over unclean spirits, to cast them out, and to heal all kinds of sickness and all kinds of disease... "And as you go, preach, saying, 'The kingdom of heaven is at hand.' Heal the sick, cleanse the lepers, raise the dead, cast out demons..."
☉ Matthew 10:1, 7-8

(To the seventy, He said) "Heal the sick there, and say to them, 'The kingdom of God has come near to you.'"

● Luke 10:9

Questions To Discuss

God's willingness to heal often seems to be in question. What do we see in scripture that indicates what the will of God is concerning healing?

Healing belongs to you, but sickness will try to come on your body. If you experience symptoms of sickness, what can you do to receive healing?

Just as Jesus sent His disciples out to heal the sick, He has commissioned us to lay hands on the sick as well. How can you obey His command to heal the sick as you reach out to people in your world?

Lay Hands on the Sick.

God has always provided healing for His people. We see this in the Old Testament, in the ministry of Jesus, and in the early church. Tapping into His healing power by laying hands on the sick is part of your ministry as a believer.

Jesus commissioned His followers to do the same works that He did when He sent them out to preach and heal the sick. In Mark 16, He extended that responsibility to everyone who believed on Him, and in John 14:12, He declared that we would do even greater works. We do His works and heal the sick the same way He often did – by the laying on of hands.

We see from Jesus that the heart of the Father is to do good and heal people. He uses us (His body) to continue His ministry of releasing supernatural power to restore health. We stretch out our hands in faith, and He works through us and gives life.

⦿ Develop the practice of laying hands on yourself and your loved ones, any time the symptoms of sickness arise. Be diligent to trust

God for your health instead of placing your total trust in doctors and medicine.

◉ Offer to pray for others as the Holy Spirit leads and the opportunities come. Don't be afraid. Step out in faith and be obedient. Jesus is the healer, not you!

◉ Use the script in the back of this book as a tool for ministering to the sick. Use the authority you have in the name of Jesus to command the sickness to leave. Then, have the person act on their faith and do something they couldn't do.

How God anointed Jesus of Nazareth with the Holy Spirit and with power, who went about doing good and healing all who were oppressed by the devil, for God was with Him.
◉ Acts 10:38

Living a Generous Life

Command those who are rich in this present age not to be haughty, nor to trust in uncertain riches but in the living God, who gives us richly all things to enjoy. Let them do good, that they be rich in good works, ready to give, willing to share.
1 Timothy 6: 17-18

It All Begins with Trust

Our relationship with God is based on trust. Definition of trust: to rely upon or place confidence in someone or something

The Apostle Paul, in his writings, instructs his protégé Timothy concerning the trap of trusting in riches instead of God. He warned him of the condition believers can easily succumb to with wealth.

The Diagnosis: Those who trust in uncertain riches have a heart condition in which their confidence is in possessions and things.

> Command those who are rich in this present age not to be haughty, nor to trust in uncertain riches but in the living God, who gives us richly all things to enjoy. Let them do good, that they be rich in good works, ready to give, willing to share, storing up for themselves a good foundation for the time to come, that they may lay hold on eternal life.
> ● 1 Timothy 6:17-19

The Cure: Trust in God. Why trust in riches when you can trust in God, the One who richly provides?

> Trust in the Lord with all your heart, and lean not on your own understanding; In all your ways acknowledge Him, and He shall direct your paths.
> ● Proverbs 3:5-6

> "Seek first the kingdom of God and His righteousness and all these things will be added to you."
> ● Matthew 6:33

Because the Father wanted to provide for us and to set us free from lack, He sent Jesus as a substitute for us so that we could live better lives and have what we needed to fulfill His plans.

> For you know the grace of our Lord Jesus Christ, that though He was rich, yet for your sakes He became poor, that you through His poverty might become rich.
> ◉ 2 Corinthians 8:9

Money is a Mirror

How we spend our money is the best indication of what is in our hearts. Since our hearts follow our money, we can look at what we do with our financial resources and see where our hearts are.

> "Do not lay up for yourselves treasures on earth, where moth and rust destroy and where thieves break in and steal; but lay up for yourselves treasures in heaven, where neither moth nor rust destroys and where thieves do not break in and steal. For where your treasure is, there your heart will be also."
> ◉ Matthew 6:19-21

Jesus warned us to guard ourselves against greed. A question to ask ourselves: Are we building God's kingdom or our own?

> Then (Jesus) said to them, "Watch out! Be on your guard against all kinds of greed; a man's life does not consist in the abundance of his possessions."
> ● Luke 12:15

Whose Is It?

God owns it all. The heavens and the earth and all that is.

> The earth is the Lord's, and all its fullness, the world and those who dwell therein.
> ● Psalm 24:1

Man is a steward, a manager of God's assets and resources. Our stewardship is not a reluctant obligation, but a thrilling opportunity to manage His funds with His heart and His purpose.

God has entrusted to us everything we have for two reasons: (1) so we can partner with Him to accomplish His purposes. (2) so we can demonstrate where our true priorities lie.

Jesus often talked about money so often because the ways in which we handle money are the most accurate reflections of our relationships with Him.

The Proper Perspective

Priority Giving: Give God your first and best. Trust Him to bless the rest.

> Honor the Lord with your possessions, and with the firstfruits of all your increase; so your barns will be filled with plenty, and your vats will overflow with new wine.
> ◉ Proverbs 3:9-10

Proportional Giving: Give in proportion to the way God has blessed you. Giving regularly and systematically is one of the best spiritual habits you can cultivate.

> On the first day of every week, each one of you should set aside a sum of money in keeping with your income, saving it up, so that when I come no collections will have to be made.
> ◉ 1 Corinthians 16:2 (NIV)

Prompted Giving: Be led by the Holy Spirit in your giving.

> Now I want you to know, dear brothers and sisters, what God in his kindness has done through the churches in Macedonia. They are being tested by many troubles, and they are very poor. But they are also filled with abundant joy, which has overflowed in rich generosity. For I can testify that they gave not only what they

could afford, but far more. And they did it of their own free will. They begged us again and again for the privilege of sharing in the gift for the believers in Jerusalem. They even did more than we had hoped, for their first action was to give themselves to the Lord and to us, just as God wanted them to do. So we have urged Titus, who encouraged your giving in the first place, to return to you and encourage you to finish this ministry of giving. Since you excel in so many ways—in your faith, your gifted speakers, your knowledge, your enthusiasm, and your love from us—I want you to excel also in this gracious act of giving.

  ◉ 2 Corinthians 8:1-7 (NLT)

The Cycle of Generosity

A principle of the Kingdom is that you reap what you sow. Generous giving is a cycle that builds upon itself over and over.

And God is able to make all grace abound toward you, that you, always having all sufficiency in all things, may have an abundance for every good work. As it is written: "He has dispersed abroad, He has given to the poor; His righteousness endures forever." Now may He who supplies seed to the sower, and bread for food, supply and multiply the seed you have sown and increase the fruits of your righteousness, while you are

enriched in everything for all liberality, which causes thanksgiving through us to God.
◉ 2 Corinthians 9:8-11

Like Abraham, we are blessed to be a blessing. We are blessed for a purpose so that we become blessers for God.

I will make you a great nation;
I will bless you
And make your name great;

And you shall be a blessing.
◉ Genesis 12:2

◉ "God prospers me not to raise my standard of living, but to raise my standard of giving."
-    Randy Alcorn from The Treasure Principle

Our motivation in giving is a response to what God has done. We don't give in order to get something from God. We give because God has already given us so much!

And my God shall supply all your need according to His riches in glory by Christ Jesus.
◉ Philippians 4:19

Jesus said in Matthew 6:21 that our hearts follow our treasure. How does what we do with our money reflect what is in our hearts and where our faith is?

God established a Cycle of Generosity based on the Kingdom principle that you reap what you sow. What is God's purpose for blessing you?

The scripture admonishes us in 1 Timothy 6 to not trust in riches but to put our trust in God and do good. How can you move into trusting God in a greater way and be more generous in your life?

Find Ways to Be Generous.

In Christ, God gave us all things that we need for life including provision for our material needs. Jesus instructed us in Matthew 6 to seek first His kingdom and His righteousness, and all life's necessities will be added to us. Because He is taking care of us, we can be generous with others.

Nothing we have is really ours; it all belongs to Him. He's entrusted resources to us, expecting us to manage them in a way that glorifies Him. Knowing that what we have comes from Him and that He owns it all makes it easier to be generous.

Giving is the opposite of the way people in the world operate. Every time you share what you have with others, you are acting like your Heavenly Father and striking a blow to the nature of your flesh. Being habitually generous changes your heart and aligns you with God's mission.

⊚ Commit to a plan for giving based on a proportion (a percentage) of your income. Make investing in God's Kingdom a priority in your budget.

● When you receive extra resources, before you do anything, ask the Lord what He would have you do. Don't assume it's all for you. The Biblical model is to give Him your first and best.

● Be sensitive to the Lord leading you to give. At times, you will feel His tug on the inside and know He wants you to share what He's entrusted to you.

Command those who are rich in this present age not to be haughty, nor to trust in uncertain riches but in the living God, who gives us richly all things to enjoy. Let them do good, that they be rich in good works, ready to give, willing to share.
● 1 Timothy 6:17-18

How To Study The Bible

All Scripture is inspired by God and is useful to teach us what is true and to make us realize what is wrong in our lives. It corrects us when we are wrong and teaches us to do what is right. God uses it to prepare and equip his people to do every good work.
2 Timothy 3:16-17 NLT

God gave us His Word so that we could know Him and understand who we are and what He has done for us. He reveals Himself through these writings and tells us the human story. As we read, we see Him unveil His glory, and we learn the epic history of our creation, the fall, and the plan of redemption. Ultimately, we find ourselves and the purpose for our existence.

The Bible is the truth for our lives, and it serves as a guidebook, a manual for wise living. To mine this truth and find His wisdom, we must study the scripture and allow it to change the way we think. If we embrace what He says, we will be transformed. We'll find new perspectives, new values, and new missions. We experience His life.

Hints for Bible Study

◉ Set aside regular time to study, and make it part of your life's routine.

◉ Approach your study with an open heart and mind. Ask the Holy Spirit to reveal the words to you so that you will know the truth and see how to apply it in your life.

◉ Write down what the Holy Spirit teaches you so you can reference it later. Journaling or making notes in your Bible enables you to accumulate notes and remember what He reveals.

◉ Look for truth you can obey. It's not enough to study the Bible. Doing the Word is what transforms your life. As you read, ask yourself, "How can I act on what I see here?"

Study Tools

◉ Look for modern Bible translations. The King James Version was written more than 300 years ago, and few of us understand the Old English well. There are many translations and paraphrases available in the language we speak today. Some versions to consider: New King

James, Amplified, New International, New Living Translation, and The Message.

⊚ The internet offers vast Bible study resources, but none are more valuable than the multitude of free Bible translations offered on site like Bible Gateway, Bible Study Tools, and Blue Letter Bible. These allow you to search passages in many translations or to find a particular scripture when you only know a word or phrase.

⊚ *YouVersion* offers the Bible app for mobile devices that literally puts hundreds of Bibles in your pocket.

⊚ If you are studying individual word meanings, a Bible concordance like Strong's can be helpful. If you aren't going to access the internet while you study, consider getting a Strong's concordance.

⊚ Many Bible commentaries are readily available. Two that you may find helpful are Andrew Wommack's online commentary at AWMI.net and Rick Renner's *Sparkling Gems* that explores the Greek origins of New Testament words. Find *Sparkling Gems* through Renner.org.

Methods of Study

◉ Book studies involve reading books of the Bible through from beginning to end. This is the best place to start with Bible study. Pick a particular book (like James or Romans) and read each day until you've finished. Make notes as you go, and look up any words you don't understand. On the internet, you can find information about the context in which the book was written. Knowing the context will bring more light to the passages.

◉ Word studies can be interesting and enlightening. You think you understand what the writer is saying, but as you study the origin of the word (or even its English meaning), you may discover truths that you've overlooked.

◉ Topical studies are a good way to research a particular subject. Use a concordance or online tool to find where that word is mentioned and compile relevant verses in your notes. Be sure to read the scriptures surrounding these verses so that you understand the context.

Ongoing Book Studies

◉ The book of Proverbs is divided into 31 chapters, making it simple to read one chapter each day. This book is a collection of sayings full of wisdom for living. The practical principles here can be read and re-read, and each time, you'll find new ways to apply them to your life.

⊚ The book of Psalms is a collection of songs and hymn and is useful for worship and meditation. The book has 150 chapters; if you read one per day, you'll read through it twice a year. Great Psalms to read frequently are 1, 23, 34, 37, 91, 103, 119, and 136.

Meditate on His Word

⊚ Joshua 1:8 "This Book of the Law shall not depart from your mouth, but you shall meditate in it day and night, that you may observe to do according to all that is written in it. For then you will make your way prosperous, and then you will have good success."

⊚ Reading the scripture is not enough to get it into your heart. You need to continue to think about it after you read, to let it stay with you and keep talking to you. Purpose to roll the things you read about in your mind and keep going back to them in your thoughts. Let the Holy Spirit talk to you about what you've read and show you how it applies to you. This process is called meditation, and as you do this, you will start seeing how you can observe the verses or see how to do them. According to Joshua 1:8, this process leads to you experiencing good success.

Resources for Giving Life

Road to Salvation Script

Hi, I'm from a church here in town, and we're out in the neighborhood (handing out waters and) praying for people. Is there anything I can pray with you about?

If they need healing, use the "Working Miracles" script. Otherwise, continue with this script.

We'll pray for that in a moment, but first I have an important question to ask you: If you were to die today or a hundred years from now, do you know for sure if you'd go to heaven?

If they answer "yes," ask why? If they answer with anything other than "Jesus is my savior" or something similar, PROCEED WITH SCRIPT.

- The Bible says that the punishment for sin is death, and the fact is that we've all sinned. Our sin separates us from God and ultimately sends us to hell when we die.

- There is nothing that we can do to make ourselves right with God. Not being a good person or doing good deeds. Not going to church. Nothing.

- BUT God loves us all so much that He didn't want us to be separated from Him and go to hell. He sent His son, Jesus, to die on the cross for our sin, to take our place and be punished for our sin. This is the Easter story.

- After He died, His body was placed in a tomb, and on the third day after He had paid for your sins and suffered for you, God raised Him from the dead.

Then ask:

Do you believe in God?

Do you believe that Jesus is the Son of God?

Do you believe that Jesus died on the cross and that God raised Him from the dead on Easter?

If they answer yes to those questions, continue:

The Bible says that believing that is not enough. We must believe - which you just told me you did - and then confess with our mouths Jesus as Lord.

Read them Romans 10:9

...if you confess with your mouth the Lord Jesus, and believe in your heart that God has raised him from the dead, you will be saved. (one benefit of being saved is that you get to go to heaven when you die!)

Would you pray with me right now to receive what Jesus has done for you and to make sure that you will go to heaven to be with Him when you die?

Repeat this prayer after me.

God in Heaven, I know I'm a sinner and I need your help. I believe in my heart that Jesus is your Son, that He died on the cross for my sins and You raised Him from the dead. Jesus, I open my heart and invite you to come into my life. I receive you as my Lord and Savior. Jesus, I accept you and You accept me. Amen

Did you mean that when you said that?

If they meant it when they prayed, they are saved according to what the Bible says. Congratulate them on receiving Jesus, and go over What Now? with them.

- Read your Bible to learn more about God
- Ask God to help you find His plan for you
- Attend church to grow in your faith
- Get baptized in water
- Tell others what you've done and pray with them to be saved

Remind them that according to the Bible, they are now saved. It's not what they do but it's receiving what Jesus has done for them that saves them.

Finally, pray for whatever needs they may have according to 1 John 5:14-15. If they don't have a specific need, pray for them to find peace and wisdom to know God's plan for their lives.

Working of Miracles Script

When someone requests prayer for an illness or sickness in their body, use this script to build his faith and lay hands on him:

Jesus went about healing and working miracles. He opened blind eyes, healed the lame, and raised the dead.

Acts 10:38 How God anointed Jesus... who went about doing good and healing ALL who were oppressed by the devil, FOR GOD WAS WITH HIM.

He did this because God lived in him and did the works through him. God lives in me because I've received Jesus, and He does through me the same miracles He did through Jesus.

John 14:12 "Most assuredly, I say to you, he who believes in Me, the works that I do he will do also; and greater works than these he will do, because I go to My Father."

Mark 16 says that those who believe in Jesus will lay hands on the sick, and they will recover.

Mark 16:17-18 "And these signs will follow those who believe: In My name... they will lay hands on the sick, and they will recover."

Are you willing to let me lay hands on you in the name of

Jesus, as His representative?

Speak to their body:

In obedience to what Jesus has commanded me to do and in the authority of His name, I command this body to be whole and well. I command you to recover. Sickness, disease, weakness, malfunction, abnormality - I command you to go. Be well and be whole.

Now, do what you could not do before. (Have them act their faith).

Has the pain gone?

Can you tell a difference? (If not, you can speak to it again.)

*If it's something that they cannot tell immediately, encourage them to thank God and get re-checked or expect a difference.

If you aren't sure that they are already saved, be sure and tell them that the God who has healed them also sent His son Jesus to pay the price for their sins. Share the Gospel with them.

The Kerysso Project is an organization committed to empowering believers to reach their worlds with the good news of Jesus Christ. We are addressing the laborer shortage needed to harvest the precious fruit of the earth – people. We believe that God wants to use every believer to do what Jesus did and continue His mission of giving life. We are continually producing resources and conducting training events in the local church to equip believers.

Visit KeryssoProject.com for more resources and contact us for information about training events in your local church or ministry.

To order more copies of the Essential Eight study guide, visit KeryssoProject.com.

Shockwave is the story of how an average Christian took the challenge to share the gospel everyday with neighbors and strangers.

Order your copy today at KeryssoProject.com.